*Studies for an Actress
and Other Poems*

Studies for an Actress and Other Poems

JEAN GARRIGUE

The Macmillan Company · New York, New York

Collier-Macmillan Publishers · London

Acknowledgments

Grateful acknowledgment is made to the editors of the following
publications for permission to reprint many of the poems in this volume:
*Antaeus, Commonweal, Confrontation, Hellcoal Annual Two, The Kenyon
Review, The Mediterranean Review, Michigan Quarterly Review, Mill Mt.
Review, The Nation, New York Quarterly, Pembroke Magazine,
Quarterly Review of Literature, Red Clay Reader, Today's Poets,* and
The Yale Review. "Why the Heart Has Dreams" and "Lead in the Water"
appeared originally in *Poetry.* "Moondial" and "The Gift of Summer"
appeared originally in *Southern Review.* The poems "Song in Sligo,"
"On Going by Train to White River Junction, Vt.," "On Actors Scribbling
Letters" (in this volume titled "Movie Actors Scribbling Letters Very Fast
in Crucial Scenes"), and "The Grand Canyon" appeared originally in
The New Yorker.

Macmillan Publishing Co., Inc.
Collier-Macmillan Canada Ltd.

Library of Congress Catalog Card Number: 72–87162

First Printing 1973

Printed in the United States of America

To Aileen,
my sister Marjorie,
and my dear friends

Contents

ONE

Song in Sligo

I had a bear that danced,
A monkey on a stick,
A dog that begged,
A cat that moused,
And, slouching by a ditch,
A rook in black of silk.
I had those birds that rode
Upon the levels of the cove
At late long twilight in the north
When the brand of sun still burned
Above the shoddy bridges of the Garavogue.
I had a boat that beat
Up levels of the reed-flagged shore
And rock-grained, rack-ruined battlements.
I had a boat and traveled with the birds
That flew against me in the breath of winds,
To each bend of the river its own mews
Of samite-backed and sable-legged young swans
Who winter from the Bay of Rosses here.
I had an island for my own one want,
A ring of prophecy and scent,
Where trees were sloped upon a moss of turf,
One ruined wall that I could sit against
And dip a ragged net to catch a fish
Of rainbowed armor in the scales of night.
I had a love who spoke to me of wars.
It was the summer of the fires.
Blackout by desolating energy.
You silken tatters of the sliding flow,
I had your voices and your leafy pools,
I have these poisons we must choose.

Studies for an Actress

(After having heard Galina Vishnevskaya sing in Dubrovnik)

What she has known, how may our hearts surmise?
Grace that is willful, wit that alerts
Misfortune that it jests with to attract
That she disarms then by a daring step,
Her heart grown richer by this peril met.
And yet a circumstance too small and tight
And she, estranged, cannot invent.
A cloudy counterfeiting takes her up,
Imbroglio of play to which she's card,
The trump they slap, the queen of restless mouth
In that quick living crowding towards the grave.

Yet turn on her the hour she's long rehearsed,
Some knife-edge of the pillaged and profaned,
She pivots on her heel and she is Faith
Like one who stands upon a balcony
Above strange ruins in rooms and streets below
That hordes new loosed like rumors from their masks
Now run upon, more dark than dream,
The which she meets with such a scorn of calm
You'd think she knew a triumph that could come
From something more than malice and than wrong
And this outfacing brings her prisoners—
Lovers who'd have their eyes put out
By such a gathered radiance.

One instant then, and she has veered
When those light things called thoughts
Solidify, grow obdurate as rock.
She flees all action now, she has gone in
Upon a demi-day that sinks towards night
Under instruction from the strangest powers
She would appease and cannot, who reveal

In the most obscure and sinking down of ways
This that they want which will fulfill
This that she does not know, which she must do.
Can she turn back? The path is overgrown.
Ahead,
Roads like lines in the palms of the dead
Now fade.

And must she be who cannot be
This that she scarcely knows she lives
Which baffles in its large, impersonal strength
(Beyond herself and borrowed from the race)
Except that she has guessed it deviously
And it takes over now and glitters out. . . .
We saw her coming, tilted on her heels
Pale her mouth, her body cast aside,
Quick knowledge made it light as any shroud

And eagerness, the rashness of a child,
Envisaging such pleasures as
Riding in a carriage in a fall of flowers
Contracted to that fine formality
That comes upon the soul when it perceives
Just what deceiving passions must take leave.

Is it a play of cross-grained theme
That she would have it that she's acting in
In an unbelievable, intemperate zone
Aloft with figures dwelling in the skies
Big-backed, with arms upraised, in stony robes,
Saluting reverberations in the clouds
Or then—the muted, trembling time
When ailing of her differences or not
She is no more than mere
Dissembling in a mirror?

Soggietto mitologico of this known theme?
Denote her history, if you will, by scenes
If that is how a life can be summed up

Except she believes her differing masks hide no one
But what the action brought to her to be
As if they were a foreign element
That she put on and then put off,
Performing in them alien acts,
The I that was another, that odd she.

And so she thought until the prince of shades
Got into the broad bed where she lay propped.
This was a nuptial scene beyond all doubt
For he would extract from her sleep-bound head
By dense green shadows laced there by a tree
The moon, the stars that grow on boughs,
The moon in her horn drawn by a griffin,
Everything eyed and starred,
Feet bounding like swallows tilting off earth,
The bounding feet of mirth

And then those figures fixed upon a point
Forever at their height and in their hour
When flushed they pierce the dragon's jaw
Or bring the severed head back home,
Who do not change thereafter, tire, nor want
For they are of the fixéd state
Of emblematic figures outside time—
That armored angel on his horse reared back
In wild-eyed excitement—

These crowd the habitations of her sleep
And are not kindly when she wakes,
Garbed figures, rapt and wrought
All to one aim and ending, blazonries
Like constellations of a zodiac
She pulls against and yet is driven by,
And she would ask these players of the immense
Pardon for her fitfulness.

And yet to all this she has come very late
And she forgets, she loses then her place.

4

We see them at the height of their excess
Who do not change thereafter, tire, nor want
And she is of the shuttling flux
That knows extinction even as it's born,
And she is sightless now with flagging search
That cannot state its end.

A leaf that falls upon a book,
An autumn of a young day come too soon,
And she has lost the thread that let
Those emblems forth, that rich connecting
Between their powers and broad awaking.
Deep knowledge dressed their concentrates.
Then had she moved in such a light of it
As if beneath their very protectorate.
Now, dying bell notes decrescendoing!

And so she falls half out of life,
Out of the net of things into the dark,
Who has no strength now for that bright-in-dark,
That second life those emblemed figures knit.
Blind fit. Nothing to hold her back from this descent
Into a void, opaque, unlit,
When out from feeling, cut the links,
Like torches quenched in sand.
And this is a kind of falling-out she also knows
A kind of hero flails. Which she cannot.
Caught now in her alternatings
Before the incessant intervenings, changings,
And this is twice-known, many-times-more-known
Indifferent death, suggestible on every hand
To light and just as soon converted to the dark.

II

There is a binding element
The which when had, sustains the crazy shifts
Of mind, the turnings and the twistings of the heart,
And those odd twins, the wish and will,

And which, when known, assembles, gathers up
All that will sustain and nourish it.
And is it this that forged the angel's smile,
The gay stone lips, the strong wings folded back,
And is it this of which the poplars speak
Glittering and shouting in the full, strong morning light
And is it this in gaunt cathedrals raised
Of shadows steeped on shadows, mountainous space?

And is it of the mind or heart?
Half human, is it more than that?
And can you give it names like joy, desire,
Like expectation, hope, or triumph known?
Is it of essence alien to the name,
Alien to time, beyond the body's will?
You seek for it, it cannot be invoked. . . .

But if it's lost, the key is lost,
The light is out, all is inert and stony,
What's loved it is not known one loves
Nor is the bird beheld, its stripes denoted,
Its savage black head with the open bill,
Its rosy-russet wings half spread
In battle with another bird
Over a helpless beetle, taken to heart
Nor taken to heart the *festoni* on the *ara*,
The godded bull's horns rising out of ivy,
The true and single government
Of the anthology of forms.

It is of the airiness of apparition
And what has not been founded on a legend?
Great cities had their start in such a light
As when after a battle someone saw
The famous horsemen, half-god brothers,
The famous offspring of the swan-loved Leda,
(The round-eyed ones according to a sculptor)
Watering their horses at a spring.
Until they came there was no spring,
They struck it forth the way they came from air,

Sign there in the Forum on which all turned
To prophesy how Fortune would grow great.

And this she knows and does not know
Assailed by knowledge of a plenitude
The dense, packed world refutes in paining ways.
The world is real, so was the spring that gushed,
So are the rough-cut stones that house what would deny
All that we see. The world is real, and are her falterings real,
And is her weakness truth, her vacillations?
That wending in between the gulfs,
That effort to create the links,
The correspondences how difficult, unfixed,
To set and fix?

And what but the mind sustains the cross-gained theme?
She judges this in that immoderate light
In which the monuments are set.
As to the stones and pillars it gives voice,
Those involutions, that crazed checkerwork
That if it or heart not open out,
Stand in their splendor mute.

She prays now to the smallest thing
Under the black brocade of pines,
She prays for the wind muffled in them,
For the fields in the shimmer of butterflies,
For valerian, dianthus, columbine,
She prays to pray, but cannot start.

Now to the violet light she recommends
When skies open into skies
That clamor of the throng of voices
Kept down, locked in, but murmurous as bees
Ready as ever for the nuptial flight,
Passionate, wholly passionate.

She prays if nothing else to be
In some dissolving medium of light,
A pond that's set to catch the arrowy beams,

Reflective and obedient as that.
She prays then to change
If it's in changing that things find repose.
She prays to praise. She prays to be
Condensed now to one desire
As if it were very life performing her.

Movie Actors Scribbling Letters Very Fast in Crucial Scenes

The velocity with which they write—
Don't you know it? It's from the heart!
They are acting the whole part out.
Love! has taken them up—
Like writing to god in the night.
Meet me! I'm dying! Come at once!
The crisis is on them, the shock
Drives from the nerve to the pen,
Pours from the blood into ink.

TWO

"*Why the Heart Has Dreams Is Why the Mind Goes Mad*"

(After seeing The Seagull *once again)*

The scent of weak lilac, cheap caporal,
The wind in the trees and the dog howling
And K loving N who loves T who loves A—
It was under those cloudbanks there
Under their weight, to meet them
The boy in a fever of grief
So shabby and rash and green
And she so imponderably of the mien
Of the tirading queen.
The boy is all wrung, unstrung,
For his mother has laughed at the wrong time.
Were he other than he, he would leave,
But the truth of her laughter is, and he knows it,
She laughs for no simple reason
And it is this rocking back and forth—
O it is not coldness that seems like shyness,
It is all vivid posturing,
Vain, reckless and melting,
Her dragonfly waist in silk,
Her tinderbox storms, flaring up
With insult worse than rebuke,
Every old hand-me-down flung down
To reduce him from fever to shame,
Weathercock fits that mutilate,
Exhilarate,
Binding the bonds more tight,

For in the next instant she veers,
Is in caressing tears,
Till crumpled at last he is brought to his knees,
To the child he was, his milky mother
So cruel to be kind whose glancing hands
Are like the touches of the willow.

Then goes—to fling himself at the piano—
A melancholy waltz
Heard all over the house—
To which they simply say as if he were the dog that howls
On moonstruck nights—
"Kostya is sad,"
Living so much in the middle of human nature
They cannot be bothered to account for its wildness.

O varied and troubling rhythm!
He knows and knows no better
That clue to the tears she can shake him down to,
Treading on all his prides
So obscurely linked to his fears.
How can he solve himself!
How can he leave this house
Rotten as cheese, a parlor for spiders,
Caught in the netting himself,
How can he manage this knotted pain
Like a retarded, retarding thing,
Himself at breakneck speed of remorse—
Foam caught from the moon
Foaming out over the keys.

O varied and troubling rhythm!
He plays in the house of aging childhood
Known to the draughty parlor,
To the flags of every dream.

Known to the woods, the lake,
The meadow where the crane still walks,
Known to the stage in the garden
Where the curtain flaps in the wind.

Known to the hour of the doleful dog,
To the mauve hour of the handsome man—
Perfumes that accost the quick-flushed cheek—
Known to candors, impulse
To what teased fancy most
Until the feelings, delicate feelings,
Are worn off.
Known to neglect and guilelessness,
Guilelessness, witlessness!
Nina, love, that smashed thing,
Nina, phantomed away,
Her candors of the stuff
To those whose feelings, delicate feelings—
Nina, wandering-witted, astray,
The varied, troubling wind
Beating, beating at the door
Until she is swept in
Like some bewildered seabird she has learned
In imitation of to become,
And he going out of the room
Really to shoot himself this time.

And you see how in the interests of truth,
The anonymous truth that respects no one,
Whether it was intended or not,
His purpose in life was to be broken.

Portrait of Four

Rueful,
Rather just always missing the right tone
Because he was retired from life,
Replete with the old apologies,
Reluctant to look at himself in the glass,
Eager after the usual encounter to erase
Its remembrance that he might glide back
Into the immune where numbed the most
He need not count over the same loss
Which was or was not the first,
Or note down the details of somebody's white Russian
Otter coat, the willful capricious, wide mouth
And that pale air of certainty
Certain riches bestow
Such as Handsome Heart who looked at her
In his taut-fitting coat,
The space between his eyes
Matched by her cat-like gaze.

Were they not old children
Breaking the rules again?
Delighted to be exceptional
Under the Widow's Window.
For them it is a secret plot they walk
Who have known the experience before
Of confronting the aging door,
The street name changed
As snow drifts over the sill,

Who early had learned how all that
Was not quite the same as the real.
Only the gap in between was where,
When lucky, they played,
She with her talent for being ill
Just when it was unendurable to endure

More of the same,
He with his language of the ideal
To banter with and gild
That when he addressed her
Made it seem he had invented her
Or at least endowed her
With a court or theatre
Of the plush and rubicund.

At times, at least, she dreamt this
On uphill streets into the strange,
Her senses strung, her pulse wan,
When she thought, if she turned a corner,
It would be seen like an animal
Alone, playing perhaps with its shadow,
And suddenly, then, the door is ajar,
There is a light at the window. . . .

He guessed this from afar
And blotted it, that pale reporter.
The artful feignings, camouflagings
He called wrong-headed dodgings,
Delinquent ruses to keep
A bandaged psyche asleep,
Bandaged since Adam.

And now he turns away
To conjure on a sofa
A disappointed man, sitting there,
One leg beneath him. Disappointed,
Glowering like an animal. His bulging, rude-red lips,
His eyes, green-gaged and merchant-small,
And springing from him rays
Like flames unfurled and bountiful.
For thirty years before he dies
He defies, defies, defies.

The Smoke Shop Owner's Daughter

The illness had wanted to kill her
Although it had not, quite.
It had left her, however, knotted and pale,
Of the size of a twelve-year-old child,
An underground child, mushroom white,
With pitted cheeks and the look
Of the one for whom it is perhaps too late
To grow up, and so who stands
Somewhere off at the start
Of the about to be and the never not.
And always silent. But then—
Speech was a thing far apart.
How could she say. It had been so long
She had been kept inside and away—
Like a child with a pointed head
Kept in bed in the slanting light
In a place cut off where they store old things,
Like a mad prince of the counterpanes—
Except that it was not so rank,
So slanting and dusty in the weak light,
Though with the dog and the cat it was cramped
At the back of the store (with her mother out front)
In the faint greys that had stayed so long
They came as close to her as a friend,
Close as the sickness, and when they went
Took what she had which was them,
Nothing more, and left her to find her way back.

You saw it there in her eyes.
Something sat there like a small thing
That having been taken away so far
Can't hear the echoes from the near
And does not know how to be
With the strange untrue of the real,
There being, neither, no one to say

If it's that or not or to try
However they might to draw her away
From the tense where she lives of the still,
No one to mend her, baffled and cropt.

Country Junction

This was the Sunday of the year's worst dog day.
Near six o'clock in the close-breathed heat,
If breath there was at all in the simmering fields
Where stringbands of the insects played too loud.
The tantrum hour, besides, of children's screams.

They loaf in the shade, old men. The cows sit down.
The train is late by an hour and now they talk,
The taut lovers with racking clocks in their heads,
Dead or nearly dead from too much life.
Too much of sameness, too, in the wilting fields,
The grass too tall, the birds too still.
Was it last night they walked in the moist dark
By the banks of syringa when the fireflies flashed?
Who saw the polar bear with its broken arm
And who the classic dipper holding the night blue up?
We've got to stick it out, who said? Have to survive,
Think of the Island, think of a month from now.

The drowsy cowbells and the broad pale river—
They broke the stalks of bitter milk.
It was the thought of what they couldn't think.
"It's not this afternoon but all of life."
Too hot to weep, too hot to know
For only time would tell they must forestall.
Dry-eyed they knew because they didn't know
Sometime they'd know when it would be too late
If something outright couldn't speak out then.

As if the outright had a place for them.
As if they worked with things said out
When all they felt much worked the best in dark.
Had worked too well? They only knew
That what was true seemed closed away from them
Or overgrown by weedy bulk that seemed like fate.

Very wish itself stillborn—unless, unless
Someone or other might slide back the bolt.

And then at last the whistle of the train
And then at last its chugging down the track.
The sun-scorched leaves, the white thick dust—
Or were they frantic passives to the face
Dead accident could turn on them?
Or—action then, to end inaction?
As the train appeared did they pray to change?
Could they imagine sudden clarity?
But how to find that if there were not love?
Yet it was love that they had gone against,
Even as they did not say but knew it
As the train's arrival freed them and one walked away.

AFTER READING

The Country of the Pointed Firs

She was the one who lived up country
Half in the woods on a rain-washed road
With a well not near and a barn too far
And the fields ledgy and full of stones
That the crows cawed over and liked to walk in
And the hill and the hollow thick with fern
And in the swamp the cattails and rushes.

It was next to living in a town of birds
But she had hens and a row of bee hives.
When her mother died, and her girl, and Joel,
She told the bees so they'd not fly away
And hung black flags on the doors of the hives
Though they'd always go when they could to the woods
Or swarm on Sunday when she was at meeting.
For each who went she had told the bees.

Change and loss was what the brook cried
That she heard in the night—but she kept snug
With crow-wood for kindling, and the sun shone good
Through the tops of the pines, and her plants
Didn't fail her, and the rosebush always bloomed
By the gnawed fencepost—what the horse had done
When they had a horse and a cow and a dog.

O there had been many, and now was there none?
Lost at sea, they said, her son gone to sea
Lost at sea they said. But if he wasn't
And if he'd come back—so she'd stay till he came
Or whether or not.
Change and loss was what the brook cried
That she heard in the night when the clock whirred.

But when the fog from the southbank came through the firs
Till the air was like something made of cobwebs,

19

Thin as a cobweb, helpless as shadows
Swept here and there as the sea gulls mewed,
O then it seemed it was all one day
And no one gone and no one crossed over
Or when the rain gurgled in the eave spout
Or the wind walked on the roof like a boy.

Change and loss was what the brook cried
That she heard in the night when the clock whirred
Just before it clanged out its twelve heavy strokes
In the thick of the stillness, black as a crow,
But no scritching now with a scrawny great crackling,
And the rain not trickling, nothing to hark to,
Not even the tree at the north chamber window.

Till she routed it, horse and foot,
Thinking of walking to town through pastures
When the wood thrushes wept their notes
And the moss was thick on the cobbled stones
With the heron wading among the hummocks
Of the pursy meadow that went down to the sea.

And she had knitting and folks to visit,
Preserves to make, and cream tartar biscuit,
She knew where was elocamp, coltsfoot, lobelia,
And she'd make a good mess up for all as could use it,
And go to the well and let down the bucket
And see the sky there and herself in it
As the wind threw itself about in the bushes and shouted
And another day fresh as a cedar started.

In Memory

Josephine Herbst
1897–1969

You believed in a world that has never come
With or without hope of this one
And therefore you would say
"I believe in what I do not see"
Insurgently or laughingly
And walked through parts of your storm
With angels of the enfranchised one
That had been truly born,
Turning the mocking cheek also:
"Who's interested now in/'Ah, wretched soul!' "
Who, indeed, in a new world
Where the heart might pulse
Fresh, disinterested at last
For everything outside itself
But where, indeed, was that,
Contradictory dissenter?
And who more full of nature,
Broad, human nature,
Who more indwelling
Than you or that loud poet
Out in the fields of feeling?
Nothing was trivial for you
Nor the angular barn in the meadow
At the foot of the broken stones.

Many selves to yourself as to others,
You did not doubt that you were beloved
And by good strangers, friends to you
Bearing the promised language.
Yet skeptic you could doubt
Out of a full heart

Who tried to beat the game
And did so, again, again,
And raised us leaves of hope by that
For something simple like a natural thing,
For something large, essential, driving hard
Against the stupors of too much gone wrong,
And by your intensity
Of flame against the dark
(You beat up flame,
You beat it up against the dark)

Gave us greater want
To change the heart to change the life
Changing our lives in the light that is changing
But which has no future, no yesterday.
O green vine on a pole,
Wanting all mingled with your own deep root,
At home with the alive as wheat,
You would have it that we may break out of ourselves,
The solitude breaking down also.
"We are now men among men, we have brothers"
Was not what you would have quoted
But knew.

In the long nights of your dreams
You were Ondine one time, you were also he
Who was hauled around the walls of Troy.
Inside was a you that lived in connections
Belonging to a thousand persons.
Putting on them, was that how you learned
What you really wore,
Which was joyful wounds, as a poet said?

Were you trusting? You did not expect to be harmed?
In the twelfth hour did you believe and hope for us all?
In the dark, what words, what signs?
Blue air of childhood, did it descend to you?

From your trials how could we not think
You would not come out alive?

Had we not seen you battle before?
And we, swept away
Almost before the door
At which loud haste knocked long,
Believed that this could be
And, too, because you'd have it so
The while a mystery
Burned its way through you.
You did not win and yet
It deeper more deeply burns
Although the seal is on the door,
Although the words go into stone.

Requiem

In the sudden white silence, where are you?
It seems I carry a letter to you, but the mouth of
the mailbox is choked with snow and the box billows,
swollen to twice its size by the thick coating of so
many flakes already fallen for hours.

I think then to telephone you, seeing a booth, its
panes pasted over and opaque like a half-marbled sentry
box. But the floor is so deep in snow that I cannot
pull the door to. Even the books are thick in it and
the mouthpiece is sifted over.

Balked, I walk into the park of the trees of this
new foliage, false orchard bewildering like a fruitless
spring. From afar strikes one bell practising to be heard.

Is it you calling?

No.   Only my heart tolling.

For J.

I think of that grave woman in the dark
There by the delicate stream at the pitch of moon,
Valor encompassed by the rare serene.
Difficult life has battered her and yet
With what magnificent strength she outstands that
No matter that the earth be dark and worn.
Might I learn, wasted and much torn,
From whence she gets the laughter of her kind.
Giving and blessing, it enkindles mind
And on the heart its wisdom without rancor fiery-earned
Bestows such light that all seems round
And brought to full, like our redemptive moon.

Dry Summer —1965

(For My Mother)

All that immense activity of thunder and lightning
For just one instant of a small
Spurt, a few dropped pebbles of rain.
And he and I so *detraqué*
And the city fetid and dusty, the air jaded,
Leaves yellow at the edges, poisoned by gases,
And your head is bad.
And your 'stratagems of the spirit'?
Not so good?
                    The big rumbling in the theatre of clouds
Like heavy furniture being pushed
Out of the theatre of the mind.
                                 Believers, those
Foreigners, those serene simpletons, gone.
A heavy sleep is like a mow of hay
And we must be tanned, tamed, and steeped
For barns of sun
                    but if the thing that said
I am your own has shifted ground?
How to get up to find where it has gone?
Has it gone nowhere but out of one
's own psychic entity or mind?
And it is teasing as the rain that will not come,
As the rumpus of thunder, as the prolix preparation
For a presentation that isn't brought off,
As those hintings, those interruptions
Of the 'revelation' that just eludes,
That from the brink will not depart,
The wings borne down by the lack of the full heart,
The 'wholeness of being,' the decisiveness of knowledge—
And I am precipitated into the summer—
Last summer of my hollyhocks—
Last terror—"Hold my hand!"

26

Our twilight talks,
She knowing, I knowing,
The unutterable gate
Drawing nearer, nearer
Through which she must enter
Without me, without anyone,
Alone,
Its approach grinding bone on bone,
Dry-eyed, both of us not trembling,
Too vast for weeping.

Out of Memory

(For My Father)

Moon and a dark stream
And I had come from long miles down the way
To the steep house of stone beside the mill
Under the bald ridgepole of the hill
By crawling tracks from where my father died
And the last quarter of the daylight sped
To stone and silence on the graveyard mound.
Rocks looked through ice like faces gouged
By sculptor's brutish thumb and then thrown down
Wild because the flamboyant ease had gone
And the delirium for perfection chilled
The while the blunt numb things looked on
Like half-done birth forms through their cauls of ice.
Death to the dreams a scathing youth
Knows better than all stones and truth,
Death to my sire. That stupor reaches yet
From where he lay there and in delirium fought
Just for the missing letter to the word
As snow fell on the partridge-berried hill,
His father to his fathers rolled,
And searched with plucking hands for *E* or *O*
And built up other ladders to the *A*
Until it seemed those letters stood like presences
Immense, fierce-eyed like messengers
Attendant with their burning faces
Upon the one that should it come
To burst in light upon the shrouded room. . . .
Beneath their staring and by fever wasted
He wrestled with the angel of their meaning
The while his mother looked from out his eyes
And on his brow his sovereign father stood.

Arrival at the Final Station

When he grew round with his hat, his blood,
The hat saw to it and the blood followed,
The hat saw to it that he bent his head
And that he trod, elephant footed.

When his moustache departed, of regal malehood,
When he began to see things as they are,
The heaviness of things, and applauded,
When the straightness dismissed the irregular

And the regular the improvident,
When all was as it had not been,
Accepted, adjusted, regulated,
When he withheld his mind from his juniors,

His juniors, his wife, his dog,
As he began to sit for his self-portrait,
Not sunken-eyed but round like a pumpkin,
When he went into silence, full silence,

The regalia of it full orchestrated,
Observing the anniversaries of those who died,
Punctiliously replying to letters,
Transforming as he adjusted,

Altering in bloodless language,
In silence then they guessed at his mind,
His juniors, his wife, his dog,
Guessed at the accommodation to

Learning how not to be
Connected with things as they were,
Excluding the measure of what had been thought
To arrive at the round ought.

Then did they say, deferring judgment,
They were learning to love him in a new light.
Not to stop loving, they must not learn that,
But bestowing on him the wrong hat,

The wrong hat, for it does not fit,
Not at all, with things as they are,
It is loving from the wrong wicket.
If it became a bloody battle then

To try to see at all
Behind his perfect Chinese wall,
They would not say in the discipline
Of the courtesy of letting alone

Of asking not, accepting. *Accepting.*
That word again.
Of obtaining a mollusc certitude
About the generosity that kills

The small, the misinformed, the wrong—
Wrong because it cannot work.
These, yes, were the problems set
To some of them by him.

His time has come, his will be done
Was what the others said.
The while he grew the heavy god,
Horizontal, manumitted.

The Giralda

(A colossal statue symbolizing faith
that is so adjusted as to turn easily
in the wind. It surmounts the square
tower, formerly a minaret, of the
cathedral of Seville)

This was all my light that while
I burned for it in a spiral
And was burned out. Then lit again
And even when burnt out, smoldering.
Think of the girasol, I spun
As even the giralda around my sun.

Faith regards its dominion of rooftiles
(O my fire burnt low).
Faith this weather vane surveying her legends
The buckled roof spanning the vaultings
The turrets of gargoyles.

Faith this dervish turned by the winds
This way and that but fixed to its spire
(O my fire, my faith turns slow)
Though handed by winds every which way.

To the north the mountains to the east the tombs
To the south the thickets of the thorn
To the west the moon that stands straight up
From the leaves of the tree of childhood.

Has the wind forgotten my weather vane
That moaned when it creaked and blew?
O my fire, it does not turn.
Something has gone down.

THREE

"*The Improbable — The Particular*
The Probable — The Universal"

No walking in those gardens
In a ring of stone queens—
Bertha Broadfoot, Geneviève—
With Love at my side
Fawning through the teeth of his pride,
All that abject surrender
The other side of a slow boil
Of hymning love turned sour
And I, divided in two,
Split-down-the-middle fool
Trying to prop up the towers
That guilty love had wrought!
I'm not doing my part!
I think too much of art!
And, scatter-brained, put out of use
By the unusable past. . . .
Like a target shot
By bristling rows of barbs. . . .
Statues, pantheons,
Even a file of rose begonias
In a kingdom of ageratum.
So much in my element
I'm out of it, it's not mine!
In a city smelling of powder,
Wine and irrelevant leather.
Thrust too much upon
A proportion "out of date,"
Outmoded courts and urns

Facades there's no point
In talking about.
An abyss divides us from the time
I'd set up in rhyme.
I'm a depraved Modern!
Deprived of the grand ideal.
No hankering is right.
Live in your time, die of it!
The addict, too, of that exile,
Another Love,
That orphan doctrine of the sphinx
To which I'd add the want
Of an elusive Fealty,
Freedom-with-honor, liberty
To come and go like air
To my royal bull's eye
Loyal, roiled center
Of the storm I'd want
Yet detached-attached, I'd have
The paradoxes met!
I'd entertain the contradictions
We admire in books, I'd make an art
Of wedding opposites that hate
And yet so attract
Impossibles declare
Nothing that's not possible.

For Jenny and Roger
(Firenze)

Drunk on your gaiety,
Your charm and crazy grace,
And drunk upon the blitheness of your words,
I talked with you all night
And now I am spent.

But I would have the play again
Of candlelight and thought,
Poems chanted, or begun
One notorious pun,
And all with such a wit
We were laughter's oracles,
And I would have again
Our carefree spirits dancing
To measures of our liking.

Hunting and fishing stories,
Arguments begun and dropped,
The maddest theories brought out
Of some old corner of a hat,
We talked the night away
Kindled by our sympathy
To wander down all rough and grassy roads,
Unfolding every vagrant plot
In which we had been drolls or gallant fools
So it might amuse.

For those who talk the night away,
What makes that pride so sweet,
That pride of life they take
In putting on the wholecloth of their thought,
Those parts they've half forgot
Of what they've lived that they play out,

34

What makes that pride if it's not love,
The heat of light and thought,
The heat of beating out
Love's steps to wine and light?

Nor is their thought known to them
Till the other gives the truth away.
They are hidden from their thought
Till the other finds it out.

Grenoble Café

At breakfast they are sober, subdued.
It is early. They have not much to say
Or with declamations fit only for whisper
Keep under pressure the steam of their joy.
She listens, usually. It is he who talks,
Surrounding her with the furious smoke
Of his looking that simply feeds,
Perhaps, her slightly traveling-away dreams
That, if you judge from her cheek,
Young and incomparably unbroken,
Are rich with the unknowing knowing
Of what he has said the time before
And with the smiles coming down the corridor
Of how it will be for year on year,
Nights as they'll be in his rough arms.

Song for "Buvez Les Vins du Postillon"—Advt.

In the Rue Monsieur le Prince
That Stephen once walked in hunger and toothache
We drank the wines of the postilion.
O I had a broken tooth myself,
I had broken my glasses as well,
And you, you had lost half your time
In the crooked streets of Spain,
But we drank the wines of the postilion.
O it was lovely at the buvette
In the time of the lilac and cherry
Not to think of the Hotel du Départ
But be drunk on the wines of the postilion
And lovely at the buvette
When a man came by in a blue smock
With a mandolin he did not play,
Yet the lilacs shook in the wake
Of the possibilities of sentiment
Of this marvelous-bodied instrument
Hung with ribbons—so svelte!
O it was lovely at the buvette
Not to think of the Hotel du Départ
Nor weep for lost causes nor why
First you must go, then I,
And O lovely to stay
In the time of the lilac and cherry
And be drunk on the wines of the postilion.

Lala and La

Now that the first flowers are out,
What shall we ever do?
Rejoice, my dears, rejoice,
And kick up our heels.

And go to look at every one
New-come from the bud.
Not yet the tides of spring
Bring blossoms from the wood.
These are the ones that dare.

Yes, and welcome everywhere,
Welcome spider threads,
Welcome waked-up wasps,
And worms that the first birds need,

Welcome green-eyed love.
The boy is about.
Come now, not one tear.
Hear these violins of air.

Nocturnes of the Birds

These nocturnes of the birds I hear
Who with icy song declare
To one another they are near,
Echoed the refrain so clear.
I call it icy. Yet it is
Ice that liquefies upon the air
With something of the haste and heat of tear
And more, the aftermark of both
In the last and stainless light
That is as brief, intense, and rare.
At deaths of day we hear them long
Make up their farewells out of song.
The woods ebb with the light they take
That they pour back then, note by note.

Elegy

O all that geography travailed.
I am sick. I have lost my desire
In the plaza of Alicante
Where there was scent from the flowers
Bushes in flower, every vine
Birds in the evening never done
The full throat of the evening open in song
Psalms of the beaches flat and white
At the end of the earth by the sea
And the sea massive with light that the masts perfect
By the shipping, the transport of ports
Of the wheat young in the groves of the olives
Darkness of olives pitted in blood
Ochre of plains by the tawny sides
Of the pepper and salt of the rock.
Palms of the Moors. By the southern fire
Rosemary we saw, and broom.
Like great fresh song the leaves start up
Under the sobbings of the light
For the cheek-enflamed in a fosse of dark.
Massed drums of the heart.
Your hard pleasure burns my mouth
I taste every light in my blood.
Before I could wring the instant out
Deduce from the light a fire
From the fire a grain—gone.

Dialogue

Dreams, said the dog,
Suffice us not.
We strain at eels and catch a gnat instead.
Who'll have Red Rabbit
And his riding wood
And my lady moon in a simpled hood?

It's perfectly true,
Said the fat cat,
I dream no more but stare at a hole
For the mouse, fiction, to come out.
Succulent taster!
Amorous waster!
All my appetite's in my paunch.

Then to your eyes he smiling said
That when we meet do shock our blood
Here's rabbit and here's dog and cat
And which is which for all of that?

The wise mistress in settled fur
Knows what original attared myrrh
Brings lovers from afar.
It is in nature, not in art,
She only has to do her part,
It's done, and both being satisfied
Cease, a family's started.

As for the dog in a net
It knows its heart
When made to quake.
Propinquity's a moment's fit.

When sun and moon were one?
Cried she,

Out of white nights grown
The wildest lightness known?

Sap of wood
And beast of blood,
World run from this
If I am wrong
When down we put our arms at dawn.

Said he,
It all depends on a lasting net
If you'd fish for eternity.

Said she,
Love's besetting property!

They Said Your Father's Griefs

They said your father's griefs on many streams
Your mother barked from out the wilderness
What times I could not count my tears told me
My dear love strode from me like iron.
Dearly beloved, that previous pact
By which a pack of ancients tolled our night
We never signed has tolled me out.
I'm in between the dragonfolds of myth
I half believe their barebones hunt me with.
Sent from the far reserves of your deep north?
Compacted ice of devil's legacy we got
By living as we did and knowing not?
Or stars have planned it thus and their conjunction
Had its prefigured smash in our small skies?
My fathers told the tale of what I am?
You foundered with your mothers in my blood?
The crazy stables of our chimeras
Exceeded half our horses', call it that.
We are such poor and unkinned lovers
Caught in the works of days half breaking down.
Say that we had no destiny but odd collusion
With how they asked the most unkind of us.

Song

Factories that look like schools
By the locks, oh by the locks
The way-worn path leads to
That the bridges lean across
By the locks, oh by the locks
Where everything looks in
On the still glitter of the skin
Of the water's membrane brimmed
By the locks, oh by the locks
That the legs of the bridge stand in
Where all is kept, the other side
Of the other look of things
By the locks, oh by the locks
Where children wave through a mane of smoke
Beyond the broken railroad tie
That the tawny grasses take
And a white tongue of water flows
By a rowboat capsized
By the locks, oh by the locks
Where I dreamed the truth of night
And spoke the falsehoods of day.

"*Aus Meinen Tränen Spriessen*"

Why did my tears fall?
How can you tell?
Our continuity is interrupted.
Nothing stays more than a second.
But they did fall, wet in your hair,
Cold on your cheek and ear.
What was I crying for?
How can you remember?
Nothing's in order.
For you I have been absent from my heart
Losing my heart in yours,
Absconded from all
To find
As I could, by indirections, past anything
To go
A metamorphosis for you.
And I did, perhaps I did,
Immersed
In the fluctuating streams of your being,
Subject to all its changingness, its original refreshingness,
Its directness and gaiety and spiritedness
And untouchable élan and wildness
And abandoned to it, almost drowned,
Speechless and sleepless to hold
You like your dreams in my arms.

In the Forest

And so the afternoon ventures into a decline,
And the world's exalted by a wind
And spiralling leaves blown fine like staircases
Turn round the descendant actor, sauntering
And gyring to the ground to go
Strained and dim upon the leaf-strewn floor
All in the moment to moment of the waftage of hues
In which perform very acrobats of rose
And the branches agile as rays on which
The carved light stilts and affects herbarium
Of sweetness, or clefts niches for the late
And distant versatility of noon.

Until across on the hill a something moves
Athwart the close-lain density of leaves
And that one tree, half scarlet and half green,
Now shadows forth a window from which leans,
Made up of light to which a darkness clings,
A being painted by the air.
I follow still its longing through the day.

Song from a Play

I did not know how it was so
But a strange life was truing me
When the cat cried for good or ill
And the rain fell with rivery smell
On the grounds of the seminary
Where the river rode by, lordly and lolled.

Blind in the world of reason,
Intractable, I would not learn
Myself must make the lauded connections
But getting burned, being ground down,

Was it that that taught me my good
When came the leaves in droves winking gold
As a wind blew, and hung the boughs
Down through the stuff of the iris-blue dark,
Strokes of the bells mulled
In between leaves so stilled
I was not hungered that while by time?

Beaucaire

It was when I was walking I came upon
A chateau, they said, of cigales
No more now than a fort of flowers
To a degree occupied by as much armies
Of plumy grasses as poppies
And bannerets of a pink-headed shrub.
How I found it was up a staircase of weeds
A limping guardian led me to
Through a gate that closed at six o'clock
(When he would show me out.)
Where they were it was dry, one was forbidden to smoke,
There were pine trees and beds of thick iris
And then the yellow ruined face itself
By a remnant wall and a tower case.
When I really arrived they were thundering,
I was abashed as if I were deafened.
There were not only sawmills in the plane trees
And tympani and assemblies of cymbals
But sometimes whole wheezing and rustling
Harpsichord companies.
Earth throbbed with the sound
As if there spoke from its roots
A thousand acres of the parched grass
And air echoing, echoing,
And distance itself aching.

Climbing the spiny stair
Of the slot-eyed tower
I saw in scantling air
Names dug deep into its walls
And place or date to make it clear
How long they wasted here:
Blancpain in fifteen ten,
In seventeen twenty Lebrun,
Vertaud, when Richelieu's cannon was loud

That did not bring these great stones down,
And Luca, who did not record the year
He carved his name for Gabrielle
In day-long dark on afternoons
Perhaps as hoarse with wild, gay din.

Cannes

I have seen those stripeless tigers
Purely tawny in their suits of tan
Climbing the sea's lavender rocks
And the lesser cats in their ivories
Undulating on extravagant legs
Their long hair like some ingenious pelt
Dawdling down their bright shoulders;
The wan sharp bones of children, too,
Like just broken-off pieces of what had been wings,
Their rib bones such small cages
For the mirthful red bird of their hearts,
And their heads sun-dusty as daisies.
But the beasts are dangerous,
Given such broad immaculate breasts
Very bucklers and very targets
For blithe arrows to strike and strike
And make bleed at least one of the rosebuds.

To Speak of My Influences

To speak of my influences:
Above all, your eyes,
And next, that jar of the bell
When I think it is you who call.
Since half the time it is not,
I have fevers to quell.
To speak as well
Of the rain in the night
We suddenly heard lying there,
That satin'd stress of a crazy wine
Silverly beating down.
That music, too, you played—
Or was it your élan,
Dense and rich? A sea-clashed mist
Warred with the wracked pulse
That danced my blood to flame
Plagued by certain notes
Of irritable brilliance and flutes
Velvet-mouthed. Ah, monotone
Of phrases faded into dissolution!
Dazed, credulous, I lived
Unbalanced by such powers
As ruled me like that speech you played
And rain's metallic waterfalls.
They ruled me, yes. Eyes kissed by eyes
And ears stunned by the delicacy
Of that fire-in-the-straw art
Wished no more than to be
Set once more alight.

To speak of my influences:
By force of fate, you said,
Who came with masks, imported more
When the suave cords were twanged,
Increased the speed at which it wound

Its flaunting silk of sound.
O heresy! All changes
Save this art at which we play,
The instant, drenched in rain,
We imitated once again
But have we the cunning to
Keep enthrallment vined?

Straw-in-the-fire love,
It's no morality play we're in,
Nor can we trick time
Nor end where we began.
Let us end as we will
While I make apostrophes
That will not more excel
Than your eyes, our dance,
And we'll love on by chance.

FOUR

A Civilization Constantly Worrying About Itself
As It Goes On Doing What It Is Worrying
About That It Is Doing

Something is definitely *not*.
Whose vices must I cultivate
Simply in order to find out
The occasion for this violent non-grief?
Am I being infected by air?
By the perpetual warnings of committees
That we are rushing swine-like like lemmings
Head on down the rocks to you-know-what
Which cannot be stopped because interest and profit
Always act too late?
But I wouldn't know, I merely live
On what I lived. Who's swimming
In my Lake Success?
How am I calling the shots for faith?
"Grand strategists are usually bad chess players,"
The shade of a woods is one thing,
The income from it another,
And their world is tomorrow
We despoil today.
Idols succeed public idols.
Once it was Marilyn, now it's—you name her.
Once Yevtushenko, now Voznesensky,
And the ugly is foremost the master,
Allaying a vertigo it escalates
With Muzak.
May only the ugly drive out the ugly?

Or are we just celebrating our sumps and our drains
Before we fall into them?
Well, cheers, old cock,
It's over my head, I'm out of my depth
And frankly right now out of my world
In a world who possibly wants
Except the mixmasters?
(Take my hand, darling,
Be not what I prey on
That preys on me, or . . . .)

Lead in the Water

Lead in the water, mercury in the air.
Too late! I hear that phrase my old love made
That taunted and that sombred and that died
On bell waves that still rock this boat,
This head. We work against such menace
Of far thunder. Each night we hear the birds,
The elephants, we see the birds all slicked
In oil, the elephants uprooting trees for water
And thousands, count them, will be shot.
Lead in the air and mercury in water . . .
Our Second Revolution's brought us this.
Those children first who worked sixteen hours a day
For their own good, so cotton capitalists said.
Ours now, we thrash in, made fat-headed
By computers, the huge and stunting. And who said:
"Over-population, over-organization"?
By this or not we lessen and we lust
The more for moon-landings, a way of death.
Escape artists, fed on swill,
Wanting more and more, forever more.
Not one "improvement" will we let go by,
Still cuddling picture postcards of the ideal,
Our hamstrung set, our soiled state
Led by the automated hyprocrite. Years like this
Of miles on square miles of the mangrove acres
Of dense-leafed forests as leafless now
As if an atom bomb had cleaned them down to stone.
But who will judge the victor? Might's still right
In this our swollen pigsfoot of a state.

"For Such a Bird He Had No Convenient Cage"

Her dreameries had been raided.
To the utmost rag and bone they had been hauled
Over the coals and up the flagpole for inspection,
To their limits they had been exposed
And all but sneeringly investigated.
Therefore what to do?
Invasions like this are of a classic port,
Our histories tell them to the last redoubt
Of unjustified sacking and not one stone left.
Hers was not of the same case.
It was not Oven Cleaner against Mace
And massed blue faces, snipers invisibly
Picking off your poor Jack, the place so broad
Hostilities had everywhere to hide.
It was not the roving muggers and armed bands,
The keeping up of nerve which means increase
Of the not-thinking or—odorous consequence
From all the crooked coldness, emptiness
That slacks the purpose in a waste of war.
It was less erect and more elect than that.
It was friends retreating into wordlessness,
Hauling in their sails, as one might say,
Like love going back on what it'd said and sworn,
Though that would numb and numb to the bone.
It was the pain of others beginning to show through,
It was *angst* about their almost inhuman bravery,
It was hearing the wound gnaw in them,
Phagocytes at the stormed body.

Free-Floating Report

At the institute of the evening of clouds
Peter Rabbit was there with the girls—
She whose pride was in her plainness,
"Her love more richer than her tongue,"
And he intimate with the nameless,
Rejoicing in its luminous influence
Like those of uncertain temper,
Such as a river.
It was a good evening, yes,
Though cold for some without their apparitions.
What disturbs, said the professor, is that people don't love
And don't love me.
And he who said: "I do forgive thee,
Unnatural as thou art."

There were somersaults and double backstands
For those strangered by an oath.
Some with light feet danced
With their heavy hearts in their mouths.
Where are the dead? asked the delicate-faced man
On crutches at the door
Who would persuade some of god.
O horsehead in a hood!
On earth as it is in heaven,
Where never the moth frets clothes.

This was no institute of wrong.
All the best impulses were brought to bear
Under the big mirrors of air.

Psalms to the irreplaceable ear, eye, and hand
Were lifted up and sung
Against the machines designed to replace them.
The oppression of steel
"profitable for all materially

and in a certain sense emotionally and spiritually"
It was thought not bad taste to question
Nor spending hours of finicking care
On making, say, blackbird pie.
For this is the way to do it!
As a tree spends a year
To produce its great head of flower.

What's the use!
I can't believe!
With whom, with whom, to go to the moon?
Was not what was heard,
Nor did the critic of the sunset step forth
Crying: can our tri-part state survive?

Inventiveness was subscribed to,
Patience, and a sense of humor.
"For this ambiguity much thanks," they amended.

Need the grand synthesizer now step forward?
They have agreed how intelligibly
Each known to the other by an image
Transpiring from his very identity

That constancia, although absurd,
Is a necessary good,
That those in the distraction of a low fever,
Having lost their original propeller,
Must be encouraged not to stall on the shore,
That in pedant paranoiac times
It is not good to emphasize
Passions like very dreams of punishment—
Hair-oil soup and gravy
Disguising the chopped-up livers of rats
After fried spaghetti.

That man going around the corner, his pants blown out by the
        wind,
That pottering, grey-faced bakery dog,
Is the observation of this to be substituted

For the dream of fair men and women?
We have come into the idiom of subways, they added.
They also admitted
That mind-beguiling conversation aided
And so did the look in the eyes
When the half-closed lids draw back
To deliver the full pulse of the light
That is like a widening in the heart,
Penetrant even to the heart's root.

Man must love and be loved.
To walk slowly in the full sympathy of noon
Is as good as beholding two trees
Leaning into one another their leaves.

O happiness! You have descended on me like a cloud!
As a bird falls silent after a well-sung day,
I shall be silent now.
Speech beyond speech—that is more to me
Than the "morn-dew" to the myrtle leaf,

Sacred to me this temporary solution
Said I.
Opposing the memory-effacing waters of Lethe
Said they.

The War Has Just Begun
(Soliloquy)

Of the difficult trek;
Not by chance being stopped; losing suddenly
Clear memory of the telephone call; keeping track
Of your many names at the single address,
The Seven,
Where the blond lives of whose color of hair
You are never quite certain. Poised
In the cat and mouse game
For the wrong one to jump out of the car,
The good one tripped, slapped
By those with as much patience as you must not lack,
You, your one mission to slip over,
Await, awake.
About what is lost you are clear.
You pin your nerve to your luck.
True, the pressure is consistent and even,
The suburbs especially you would like to avoid,
It is here that they disappear the swiftest,
When you go to knock at the door
That the stranger answers.
Clues broken. Or is this planted?
Walking, looking for birds with a message. That dove!
Cognizant of the Ark? If Jorge
Fails to appear at the *Jardin des Plantes*
A part of the web is cut.
Lives hang on the tissue of knots, interconnecting threads,
Death to your sort
If misinformed by the scrambled words.
Act, damn you! It is this you were meant for
Opening the door to the sweating shadow
Quickly, quietly, in the structured maze.
In the structured maze *they* have structured?
But criminals of your own gut, the will coming apart,

Are always at the next corner.
Not driving a hundred miles in the snow
Past the hooded peasant women
To warn the boy of the wrong turn,
Meeting no more at the stations, sitting down
Like a preoccupied passenger waiting for a train
To exchange the necessary words,
He leaving first, you after.
The camouflaged hero performing the camouflaged act,
A part of somebody else's scheme, about to become a thought
In somebody else's mind? But it is also you who foresee and stall,
Triggered on the tight rope,
Who have had a short way with the threats;
Even in the silence of the Committee
Almost the hint of something too vague to name,
Reservations that could become the neighbor
Of something that might become distrust—
Something stealthy and hid
Kept you going, alert
With the constitution of a dog with a good nose.
It being your provender or not
That the trail is inexhaustibly long,
That you and the others are in a grand fugue
With no point of termination, continuing its contrapuntal
      involutions
Without ever having to come to a logical point of rest
If the cords are tense,
That the connection between you and dead Juan
It is up to you to carry on—act for his act
Of risking and losing. Suppose that Ramon
Who vanished is living and you will get through to him.
Suppose! It is not entirely a fiction
If we live by fiction, if we keep up to the mark
For the sight of the quai
Reflecting that something we cannot say
Have we not known it before?
We have not. It is what we would know.
And if, in the many-eyed labyrinth
You come to the moment you can no longer avoid,
Then, without blunder, to meet

What you have traced over and over in sleep,
The map of the rivers, the vines, the walls,
The walls with the windows in them.
To be in the windows, to have the design
Of the thing you have lost suddenly clear,
Pressing against you,
Then breaking out
Into the whole sight
And your half-finished life finished in it.

Resistance Meeting: Boston Common

It is Spring in the Common.
We are among friends.
The smog of confusion has lifted.
Now may light shimmer from the tree,
Now we need not go mad on abstractions
about Power, Fire Power, Garrison, Arsenal
Fire Power, Power, Poseidons
(giving a "multiple warhead Navy Missile" the name of a god)!

Now is Deceit not the General
nor Equivocation the master of tongues
as the firm-voiced speakers speak,
laying it down in a way that is clear,
every word counting, explicitly, sparely,
the clarity being the astonishment,
pricking up the ears, alerting the heart,
though we, incidental among the hundreds at ease all over,
are not the target of aims
nor are we in the toils that have seized whole forests at once.

April in the Public Garden.
The boys who will be drafted are here,
some bearded like disciples,
others with the large dark eyes of *The Volunteers of 1792*
as painted by Thomas Couture,
horsemen-like as a painter might see them,
stilling, instilling their fire
of so much being to be praised by the future.

No point in going on about handsome people
with their thick hair glittering in the wind
about which we have had much comment from ads
so that we are less free to think of Titian's *Man with a Glove*
or a Degas portrait of some olive-skinned pride,
the élan of the painter and subject met at the point of imagination

where the magnificent being
garbed in the full dress of his civilization
completes in himself by his beauty
the rose of every expectancy.

For those lounging and lolling here,
what painter will arrest them in their gear,
at their height of time?
Not hardened yet or tarnished, standing yet
upon the grounds of choice,
still at the moment of decision
or at the moment before decision.

April in the Public Garden.
Also glittering are the hides of the horses
that the policemen sit on like Order and Reason
which is not unlike the order and reason of superior fire power,
the order of Poseidons and nuclear umbrellas,
the talked-about order of seabeds to be used for launching pads

which is not of the order that the speakers are speaking
in spite of the iron order of defense systems (one already
        obsolete)
dug into mountains so deep it is a whole way of life—could
        survive
a direct hit for thirty days—

An order it is news to hear of in the open air where public
        persuaders
usually slide from "fourth class nations" to "regardless of race,
creed and color"
for the good of the manipulated, card-indexed,
if we are to believe what we read about the faceless ruled by
        the faithless,

An order that has always been known,
known, forgotten, denied
under the pressure not to distinguish what is true from what
        is necessary,
flying the flag of expediency,
which is the mere power of the mind

or the idea, the pure idea of man
witness on his own terms to what he knows,
making and re-making what he is.

Panting dogs run free from their masters,
and when the applause thickens
in the animal excitability of those who have not lost faith
in the light that is mirrored for which all thirst,
or are said to thirst,
join it in a salvo of barks

as the speakers continue to speak of an order
other than the mere boast of the megaton
which is of the stung resolution
of the integrity of being
fully to resist, dissent,
to take the difficult step,
"choosing with all of your lives,"
to bring to bear
energies dispersed in fall on fall.

All this on a bud-gemmed day whose luster
the words of the speakers do not wither,
trying to say the honest thing
about the hard thing to do:
resisting with what doesn't give way
in an hour or a day:
going to war or jail,
hiding in churches or Canada.

April in the Public Garden.
We have heard the message, they have not departed,
for the rain does not fall with the same prickling on us;
it is not we who must weigh
the passive acceptance of a code
against the conscience—or else—
nor shall our blood enamel the pages of the book of some life,
nor are we expected to become heroes (or anti-heroes)
by dispersing the jellied fire
and the chemicals depositing arsenic in the soil.

On Going by Train
to White River Junction, Vt.

(The Connection Severed in 1966)

It interferes very little
As it lays down its way.
When it needs to, it follows a river
But does not prevent the roots from their water
Nor by the smut-faced boulder
A small stream from joining a larger,

Nor smashes up hills nor halves them—
Roots and the intricate indwellings thereof
Exposed, and the earth become mud,
Oozing and bleeding away—

Nor removes ledges of sunlight
On cliffed parallels of rock
Nor savages nuances of meadow
Nor rips away mosses in a hollow
Nor requires that sawn woods stand like so many scorched
      matchsticks
Nor musters out ranks of cornstalks
Nor engorges great swatches of dingle
Of ostrich fern in the blue-heroned swamp.

You travel with it and the stones by the river—
By the tussocked meadows

66

With ponds set glittering like an eye
In the fine lashwork of twigs and boughs in a tangle
Continually nourished so near their mother
By the long runs of sweet water—

Its course neither mathematically severe
Nor of the convenience of martial order.
The scrolls, the cartouche of mists, wisps,
Breathings in crooks and bends
Fume out from a hill undismayed by the disarrays of so
        much unfolding,
Discontinuous flowing

By the green baize of molehills, of ridges,
In pastures the serene flanks of white horses,
Under light that dazes and deifies
Cows winding in among eskers.

The Grand Canyon

Where is the restaurant cat?
I am lonely under the fluorescent light
as a cook waddles in her smoky region visible through an open
      arch
and someone is pounding, pounding
whatever it is that is being pounded
and a waitress cracks with the cowboys lined up at the counter
lumberjacked, weathered and bony
intimates, I would guess, of the Canyon,
like the raven that flies, scouting above it,
of the hooked face and the almost flat sleek wings.

Where is my cat? I am lonely,
knocked out, stunned-sleepy,
knocked out by the terraced massed faces
of the brute Sublime,
color inflamed,
when I came to the edge and looked over:
violaceous, vermillion
great frontal reefs, buttes,
cliffs of rufous and ocher angles,
promontories, projections, jutments, outjuttings
and gnarled mirlitons, so it seemed,
twisting up out of depth beyond depth
gnarled like the juniper tree
rachitic with wind I hung on to
as the raven's wing, glassy in the light of its black,
slid over me

there at the edge of this maw, gash
deepest in the world that a river has made
through an upwarp in the earth's crust,
thickets of tens of thousands of gorges eaten out
by freezing and thawing, tempests, waterspouts,
squalls and falls of the river

with its boulders, pebbles, silt and sand sawing down
through the great cake of geologic time,
eight layers laid bare,
the total effect creating what geometrical effect
in a rocky silence so clear
a bird's voice, even a boy's
is spunged out, sucked up by this stillness
stinging, overpowering the ear,
pure condition of the original echoing soundlessness
this voluminous wrung resonance
welling up out of the handiwork
of the demiurge wrestling down there
in an infinity of imperceptible events
some ten million years,

ages blanching to think of,
taking the switchback trail,
slipping and sliding,
forever slantwise descending
into new confrontations of parapets,
chimneys, mantels, segments of angles,
modelings of rock of slacknesses and accidental tensions
combined with the effects of its weight—
the total effect never total for never can you see it all, not
      even guess
at mazes of the proliferation,
and the river will not be visible
except from a driven angle,
the snaken twists of its rapids looking petrified, frozen
from the distance of a deep mile:

somebody saying a mountain could be plucked up by its roots
and dropped head-first down there and it wouldn't dam up the
      river
so that the waters would run over

and that the Washington Monument could be kept out of the rain
under one overhanging of an otherwise vertical red wall
where the gold of the light on that chaos of creases nervously
      darts

like the violet-green swallow stitching its leaps and arcs
over the gliding raven,

over the camber of columns, tawny rotundas of ruins
writhed, mottled, crested with shells,
escarpments
downbeaten by frost and rain,
parallel rangings of
rostrums, pulpits and lecterns,
and the mad Tiberius arches groining
cave holes on cave holes in the same wall of limestone, red
from the ironstone drippings,

Aztec pyramidal temples rising in hundreds of steps
to the summit of the seemed shrine
curtained, girdled with snakes and necklaces of hearts,
wet with sacrificial blood,

rusticated building blocks jutting out in warlike
        ramifications of forts,
stockades of black frosted rock,
towers of the baldness mounting like obelisks,
pyramidal forms from the sands of Egypt,
crags vertiginous, cupolas, alcoves,
amphitheatres, arenas, organ pipes, flutings,
porches of rock, wedges of shadow in perforated rock,

and the gold of the light nervously darting
on the Bright Angel shale, pink with long stripes,
on the lavender blue of the Shinumo Quartzite,
on the deeper rose of the Hakatai shale,
on the blond Coconino sandstone
riddled, it's said, with the trails of sea worms,
on the grey Kaibab limestone
with casts of shark teeth and horn coral imbedded
like the Hermit shale of the topmost formation
with footprints of salamanders, insect wings four inches in
        length
and even a dimple left by a raindrop during some era of burning
and hailstorm, torrent and drought,

era on era stacked here,
untold era on era,
as the eye like a long-legged insect on a windowpane
slithers and shudders up and down
the banded and ribboned, ribbed systems of rock,
into and out of shadows,
chromatic world of what glitters like phantoms,
corrugations of scaffoldings appointing to chill
over the continuous surface,
assemblies of aggregations
sand-pocked and pitted,
ridged, wind-serrated,
tawny threshholds in the lying out there of the steeps,
in the drinking up of the stillness
pressed in by the gorged rock
deepening in the light of the motes of beams
under those clouds that like water lilies
enclose within them this silence received
that they graze upon and are gone.

Grief Was to Go Out, Away

Grief was to go out, away
From this bedside of cliffs and shells,
Awakings in mornings to white-raged manes
Hoisting themselves up over rocks
And the white mother of foam sped
In a thickened broth curdled white
Back to the throngs of the oncoming rigors.

Grief was just in the having
Of so much heart pulse gone out and away
Into absence and the spent shadow
Of what ran from our fingers as ripples
Of shadow over the sand and what eluded
In a bending of mirrors the tipped tints and reflections
And was just so much running down the packed sands'
Mile-wide blondness of bird-tracked floor.

Was to behold in leaving, as if for the first time,
The fair-weathered crown of the mole
And the light chained to the grass-scattered peak.
Between the gates of the bullet-round rocks
Was to pluck up by the roots the salt hay
Where the seaweed lay wine red
And the foam was combed with gushed red
Was to leave carrying sealed in some envelope

Commandments instructing through leagues down
Where all must be seen through the hidden,
Through shade upon shade, down through layers,
Where all must be seen suspended in the stilled inner scene,
And the word must guard the deed and the inner word
Must not spill its center of smoke
Or break out from the windows of music
Playing deep in the night no one may arrive to

While you come back to your life
In a strange grace of gratitude,
Loving the least and most meagre
Of the held to, the unchosen given,
For here stand the encircling premises
By which don't they leap from, the distances?
And even as in the beat of the running foam
The enhalting power of the thing
Crowding the mind, pouring over the eyes?

Is it in the poignancy of tests
That we strike fire at the source,
At farewell that we clasp what we know,
And as if it were dying, run to embrace
Our life lying out there, misadventured, abstruse,
In the great wedge of light beamed forth—
Like messengers sallying out
To your "I see! I see!" bearing a scroll
On which the word is almost decipherable.

Attempting to Persuade You to Go
for a Walk in the Public Garden

It was so pleasurable,
I wanted it to be so free,
I wanted to be talented for life
With the stamina of a rocking horse
Walking with you out of the dust
Of our bookkeeping duties.
The common daylight I wanted
In a company of others under the plantains,
Park-strolling by the pigeons
Of rainbowed necks under the lindens,
Tress lengths of the willow
There by the toy temple,
By the Camperdown elm shaped like a girl,
By the Belgian elm and the oak,
That parasoled "sweetheart tree,"
Its green rind overwrought
By boasting heart on heart.
I wanted it not especial,
The sweetness was in the usual,
Merely the swan boy as he pumps
The bicycle pedals of the boat
That glides at a cortege-like purl
Solemn with children, heaving with mothers,
Merely the civil order of statues—
General Washington on a horse
Apple green, of corded chest,
And Edward Everett Hale about to get
Out of his stone to take a walk—
Under the long-reaching boughs of the beech to be
Disarmed by its knotty intricacy
As two gloved women are
                              who remark
Upon its fine-grained bark.

I wanted what the day was,
The prophet bird, auguries
Cast down by a branch of leaves,
Merely the simple and natural,
The slightly euphoric and free,
Trees named that we might learn
About more kinds than one,
Stone examples of the great
Or at least not insignificant
To remind us of something more
Than our trivialities.
It was the idleness of leaves
Knee-deep from the waftage of other days
Coming into the eyes
And those we met, adrift
On esperances, reveries,
Those worlds locked up in all our heads
Of visages of memories
Particular, unique, unknown,
Yet ancestral as a cloud
We move from, half unknowing
Till a waking sleep is torn.
It was the garden feeling,
It was the Eden good
Here by a lawn of water come
Upon it, to touch us,
Touch us, and let befall,
Stung into fire,
Helpless desire.

The Gift of Summer

Once more, my love, once more
I am where you were
When midsummered, you wrote
Outright on my heart.

Once more these open fields,
This wood, once more the paths I paced,
These birds, the kith of grasses,
Trees in a tremble long

From tendrillings of the wind.
Once more, my love, once more
By these waters over stones
Whose tumult richer tells than I

My twice untold confessional
And I am halt again to say
How this shadow-figured lawn
Was ever figured then

By how you might have come
From out the leaves, half made
By the sun and shade,
The issue of my mind

Upon such senses fed
As you had learned and owned,
Composer of this summered thing,
The musk of air and moon.

That you should love me was the summer's gift
Incredible I took for truth
That fed so on the flowers I grew faint
With increase of their light

And thus did learn to live
And by that rarer breath believe,
Prodigally by its excess
To take a wonder as my faith.

And once more now, once more
Walk where time past time
Underneath these moody aisles
You ever were about to come

Although the wind now wakes a storm
Of leaf-loss, old rue
Of autumn's monotone,
And all is masked by flying rain.

And yet this cloudy ground
Is still so bound around
By how the stewards of my faith
Rapt me by their heady proof

That the rain-dried, smoked-off scent
Of lilies and of iris is still pent,
And clustered is the field
That sits across the way

With the blond grains' light.
A fragrant drowsiness is kept.
Kept the waters' cries
That twine upon your name.

O setting forth and starting out!
Kept the dazzle and the ache
Kept the suns of marigolds.
It seems I see you start

With these, under the intricacy of boughs.
O keep, keep, cast not out.
Be adamant, you powers,
And be me steadfast, hours,

To what I richer learned
Than that you fail and fade.

SIX

Motifs from the Dark Wood

I

My love was stolen from me,
Carried away like raw youth in a coach
Sang the dying voice of the morning
By a black shed where a bird was caught,
Fluttering and clawing, its eye
Liquid with the glycerine of crying,
Its low warble as it strove webbed-over,
Caught in the threads of that stooped porthole
That gave on the east, sea of cloud,
Where the sanguineous carnation of the late-wintered sun
Reached out to lay its blood
On the blood of the bird,
The dusking webs inflamed by the rays,
Inflamed by the rays as by blood.

Like our childhood troubled in the lost park
At the coming of night on a low-clouded evening
And the slowing down of the rhythms
In the paling of light and the quieting
As the edge of the wood thickens
Into which the vespers of small green voices
Have huskily entered and halted . . .
Coming from meadows at sunset
Seen through the tarlatan of blossom
How slow our walking, our pausing,
Dawdling over the bridges
By water winding through rushes.
Outbursts of voices! A sudden star!

Can we ever not linger, delay . . .
On a pond of moon that lolling sail
May flare us out on a far journey . . .
Rifflings and ebbings, departures . . .
Your hand on mine unsettling me
As music would a tree.

II

The brambled chase in the rides of the forest
As the wind blew its hunting horn.
Following after its notes under leaves,
Through the down-reaching boughs of fir,
Parting our way through them and briar,
Till we came to the twilit avenue
Of trees in ill-set rows
By a brook engorged, gone green and broad,
And the passage of whispers done.

Was it here we dreamed we saw
In a round-centered point like a grove
A spreading-antlered stag and doe
Beside a shaft of stone fenced round
By sparse, rigid iron
And further palisading it
Rivals as of unknown flowers
Blanche-tall but crimson-mouthed.

It was like a chapeled grove
So wan the light come down.
Set deep in moss the name
On this neglected thing.
Abruptions of a light
When an eddying wind might bring
A kind of shudder back . . .

And what begins again,
What begins, who tries to speak
As if through webs upon the mouth,

Who begins, who tries to speak
As if through other lips
Begins to and despairs,
Begins to and cannot.

Moth! What has happened!
You that appear!
O in the wood wept
Drawn on by that fey...

Thereafter into the dark
Who has eaten of the bird's heart.
At every seventh step a drop of blood
In the middle of this square of wood.

Moondial

To speak of this hot day: the flaming fields
Filled to the brim with scorch, tasting of singe
And bake and brown: those gasping trees, some dying
At the top: a tangle of long-legged flowers,
Their faces put askew upon their stalks,
And Queen Anne's lace as slant on crooked stems:
Earth ribbed to a near extreme,
Balding of grasses burnt and white with dust,
The lank weed bitten with zest:
Flight, erratic, of the ill-trained grasshopper
And butterflies who test what flowers are left,
Riding them down from prong to prong. . . .
And what with this thin harsh and hacksaw whirr
Of insects that succeed the soft-set song
Gritting and grinding like the shears of time
This last of summer lags
Where cobwebs keep their dusty disrepair
On bushes sere and crackling, juice of leaves
And moist hues gone, all gone,
While on their stalks the flags of leaves hang down
Limp and sapless on the pithless stem
And somewhere else the frazzled leaf has shown
This young tree turned to russet, starved for drink.
Sahara flames
Upon the tracked and rutted, bare-bit ground
Where feet have trod it to a kingdom come.

Into this parched land I come, to the long
Starvation by skies, while in my heart's
A counterpoint—
You know the road so splashed by shade
And then so trodden white where the moon fell in
The dialog made for mild delirium
Not unlike the contagious jubilation
Of these small stringsmen of the grass

Who pluck the long high C.
And then that moon that stared us blind
Or me.
And I would cross by battling stones
Those streams we did of fumy mist,
Against the unremembering surge, to take
The reversed step, and plunge again
Into the vanished silvers without name,
Dazzle of the soft sound of small winds,

And without sanction now to speak that speech
The great night took from us or let us think
We spoke, however wordlessly,
Though you'd but live therein and bask with me
On the lip of the moment, deep brow of the hour.

We walked in moonstuff, lawn and tissue of it,
Past forests chained by it and molded so
That levels of its fountains of dark growth,
Tier upon tier of rich, broad-plated leaves,
Were sculptured by the massy flood,
Fey governor of the insubstantial.
While certain trees, the locust and the walnut,
Were so exposed to all that clarity's balm
Each semi-tropic, half Italianate leaf
Seemed so defined you'd think a draughtsman's pen
Had cut it out of air. Serene, precise
Illumination of the form—
Bleached by light the serrate leaves
On urn-shaping boughs.

And walked we by the harvests of the light,
By meadows where it lay so heaped we might
Have gone to gather it and toss the stuff
And play it out like spray or tuft
Or dip our hands in it to the wrists.
And walked by over-arching boughs, down grass-rimmed roads
Where darkness comes to settle in again
And build its tenebrous structure shade on shade.
A bridge somewhere in middle, made of motes,

Is swaying in the windless air
And as you look again it shifts,
Twinkling and flickering on the still-bound earth.

And then by pastures where it browsed,
Our blameless phantom, till it mixed
With sheep unshepherded and cow,
Heavy-breathing, pulling at dim stalks,
And horses starting up,
Their hooves belling on the drum-hard earth,
Snuffling and tossing out their manes flung dark
Upon the supernatural substance of the light.
And doors in forests leading into doors,
Some bannister of air down that steep hill
Set thick with boles and heavy-hanging leaves,
A snail-shell spiral coiled from out that press
Of traveling loomed and sweet evaporate.
And thus she ascends, descends,
Making her acres everywhere
When from the press of shadows we come out
Into the full untutored dazzle lying bare,
Hills rounded on hills, cobweb sewn.

Myth-making mist and resurrecting light
How still and calm and yet the vapors toil
Up flank and crest to erect their castles there.
Nothing of this will burn us. It is wet.
And yet there glitters up a signal bough
Crusted with diamond dryness or just blanched
Into a great stark bone of flower.
But in the valley such a seethe of foam
You'd think the glitter broke into a song
Too faint, though, for grains of light to carry.
It bore along the nerve and under skin.
We almost could not hear it so we sang.
We were animals of the moon
We stood from out the thatchings of the leaves
In the full gaze as they who would defy
The two-in-one, the life and dying of it.
Its tumult trilled the vein of every thing

And dressed the trees.
Perfect they stood and were the more perfected
We thanked the light for falling as it did
To show their every tangle in the whole
Of wildest, most cross-flowing intricacy.
Such wildness asked for ceremony.
We rose and then we danced a formal tread
Of measure to the trees that graved
Their wilderness upon the thing
Within ourselves that drank it in
We drank the air that drank of moon,
Deceptions that it practised—or were they
Intensifyings of the way things were,
Crazings to the blind who see they see
Or think they do? It flows upon them,
They are washed in curd,
Original essence they say they've fallen on
It is too fair, it bewilders them,
Their senses thrash, they behold, they die
Into one another, into grass, the wanderer airs,
Dying would not ask to be reborn.
There is a moment on the moondial. It has come.

And must the moon thin and the light grow dull
And all that dazzling sunlight of the dark
Be strained through gauze for nothing?
Must the small-eyed spider strike down the wall
For slow murder of a moth,
Fireflies, their lights working on and off,
In fetters of the caught?
And must the dawn wear the world away
Of mystifying touch in twining light
When by a window flows the night
Die to the mind as the light goes out
And the wings open of day and you perceive
A slaughter of innocents—
Some long antennae or a gossamer thigh—
Fragments of the ephemeras.

Mad are the questions that a blindness woke,

A waking up like blindness to all else.
Must I beg to be washed of the moon dust
As I soothe the enfevered flowers of fissured earth?
A bird turning a corner in a wood
A star that glides into and sifts the leaves
A blade of grass that stirred in sleep
To startle us—as if with noise!

I raise again these moon-splashed fields,
Like half-remembered legends I recount
How apparitions skeined us in a coil
Where wholly given, wholly found,
Our beings' threads were wound.
Secessions, then, by sun!
But not from the One.